A Quiet Corner Of England: Studies Of Landscape And Architecture In Winchelsea, Rye, And The Romney March

Basil Champneys

In the interest of creating a more extensive selection of rare historical book reprints, we have chosen to reproduce this title even though it may possibly have occasional imperfections such as missing and blurred pages, missing text, poor pictures, markings, dark backgrounds and other reproduction issues beyond our control. Because this work is culturally important, we have made it available as a part of our commitment to protecting, preserving and promoting the world's literature. Thank you for your understanding.

A QUIET CORNER OF ENGLAND.

STUDIES OF LANDSCAPE AND ARCHITECTURE

IN

WINCHELSEA, RYE, AND THE ROMNEY MARSH.

BY

BASIL CHAMPNEYS, B.A.
ARCHITECT.

WITH NUMEROUS ILLUSTRATIONS BY ALFRED DAWSON.

SEELEY, JACKSON, AND HALLIDAY, 54 FLEET STREET,
LONDON. MDCCCLXXV.

ST. THOMAS' CHURCH, WINCHELSEA.

CONTENTS.

	PAGE
INTRODUCTION	7
CHAP. I. WINCHELSEA, RYE, AND THE ROMNEY MARSH	9
II. WINCHELSEA	14
III. RYE	27
IV. RYE CHURCH	38
V. THE ROMNEY MARSH, THE ROMNEYS, AND LYDD	51
CONCLUSION	62

A QUIET CORNER OF ENGLAND.

INTRODUCTION.

THIS work is the result of a few days' visit to the south of England made in the early autumn of 1873. It does not pretend to exhaust any one of the subjects involved, nor to rest upon other knowledge, technical or historical, than what is readily accessible to any visitor; but simply attempts to convey to the reader the impressions which the several objects made upon the mind of the writer. It makes no claim to any theory or system, nor to any leading idea, unless it be a conviction that in the study of the works of nature and of art system and theory are better absent, and that such things speak most truly and most powerfully to those whose position towards them is both passive and catholic—uninfluenced by any analytic theory or exclusive limitation.

One aim the writer had definitely in view: a jealous desire that the modest and homely landscape and architecture of our own country should receive more general appreciation. It is, perhaps, not the least of the penalties which we have to pay for the elaborate civilisation to which we are born, and for the specialisation of the several aspects and functions of life which is one of its conditions, that our minds are less open than in earlier and simpler ages to those subtile influences of nature and of art which thrive upon daily and hourly association, and which move us more slowly and more unconsciously, but not less effectively, than those of a striking character. The centralisation, the engrossing business and consequent restlessness of contemporary life, have made it difficult for all, impossible for many of us, to realise the necessary conditions of sensitiveness to influences so delicate and so tranquil. Meanwhile the importance both of nature and of art as elements in human life is, in theory at least, abundantly recognised. It is for this reason, I believe, rather than on account of any essential superiority, that the more imposing forms of Continental landscape and the more colossal productions of foreign architecture are so commonly preferred in the present day. Those whose association with either landscape or art is more or less occasional, naturally find grandeur more effective than modesty, scale more easy to appreciate than sentiment. But such emotions as are engendered exclusively by gorgeous effects are apt to be sensational, and are neither so wholesome nor so enduring as those which arise in a quiet and homely atmosphere;—moreover, familiarity with the more specious is apt to render the more modest permanently insipid.

It is impossible to test the relative value of English and foreign architecture by any standard but that of individual feeling. Whether it be the result of familiarity or of hereditary association, it is certain that, for me at least, the more homely and vernacular old English buildings possess a poetry and sentiment which I can find in those of no other country which I know, and in this feeling I imagine I do not stand alone. Whether this appreciation is absolute or relative is a question for psychologists. For the practical artist it is enough to know that it is likely to be shared by the majority of those for whom he works, to many of whom reproductions of foreign styles must be strange and void of association.

The restlessness of the present generation is not confined to passive habit and mood. Would that it were! We are so generally given to manifesting an exuberant activity in the destruction of ancient beauty and the substitution of modern abominations that there is reason to fear that contemporary sentiment may shortly become universal, when it shall have swallowed up all monuments upon which other feelings might be nurtured. Moreover the finer poetry of architecture is so tender a growth that it can scarcely survive even the proximity of the obtrusive vulgarities of modern days. Here and there only, in out-of-the-way places, in quiet villages or remote country towns, it still lives uninjured; and from these, if at all, it must be derived and propagated.

The tract of country which is here described is one which retains more than almost any other which I know the sentiment of a past time, and it is on this account that I have chosen it for description.

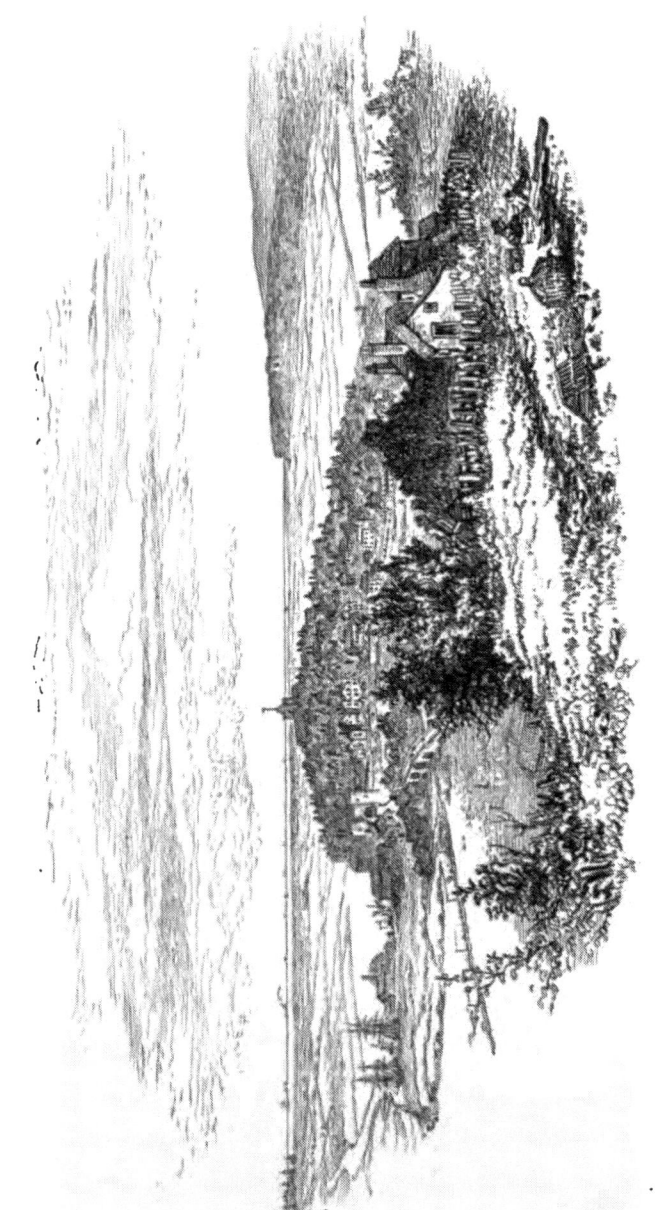

OLD COAST LINE FROM RYE TO WINCHELSEA.

I.

WINCHELSEA, RYE, AND THE ROMNEY MARSH.

WINCHELSEA, Rye, and the Romney Marsh, contain an infinite number of historical associations, for all of which the reader is referred to many valuable guide-books. If his ambition leads him to go deeply into this branch of the subject, he will find Holloway's 'History of Rye' quite an ideal of voluminous dulness, and a little research will no doubt bring to light abundant additional material of similar quality. Our business is merely with the actual objective aspect of the country and of its monuments, and with so much of historical interest as these suggest by internal evidence, or as they necessarily involve.

To the north-east of Rye is a windmill on a hill, from the top of which I saw, one brilliant day in early autumn, one of the most interesting and suggestive views which could be found in this or any other country, of a part of which an illustration is given opposite. To the extreme right are the Fairlight Hills, towards Hastings; nearer, but still to the right, is the ancient city of Winchelsea. The promontory on which it stands is almost covered with wood, and in the distance no building can be clearly seen excepting the Land Gate, through which the main road passes, winding round the eastern side of the hill. Immediately in front of us is Rye, with its pyramidal grouping of picturesque roofs at all angles and at every level, leading up to the squat tower and stunted spire of the church, crowned by the weathercock, the apex of the pyramid. Over the left shoulder of Rye, scarcely discernible, is Camber Castle, and in the distance to the left is the Port of Rye, with its few low, straggling buildings, and its little church and group of masts. Between the port and the city runs the river Rother, which to Rye is the river of life, the link between the present and the past, the one differentiating cause between Rye, the Cinque Port of the living, and Winchelsea, the Cinque

Port of the dead. To the left, beyond the extreme limits of our illustration, stretches the great Romney Marsh, from which the towers of Lydd and of New Romney stand out in the clear distance. The flat monotony of the Marsh, the bed of a recent ocean, the '*mare velivolum*' of Cæsar, which a few touches of the pencil could make into sea once more, fills the landscape between the sea-line and the prominences with an equality of level which is almost fluid, up to the *actual* verge of the channel. But the more ancient and more evident sea-line skirts the hill on which Winchelsea stands, curves inward and comes almost under us in a well-defined bay, is lost to view behind the city of Rye, to which it clings, and again behind the shrubs and cottages of our immediate foreground till it meets the wide bay to the right, leaving Rye an island with a narrow channel on the north side, and then passes beneath us at the bottom of the cliff to the left, and so into the infinite regions which lie beyond all vignettes. Looking at this well-defined line, at the features which recall the original conditions of the landscape, at the arches that bridge the high tide, the gate to supplement the defence, with the sea-channel for a moat, the abruptness of the sea-worn limits of the two promontories, it needs a strong and deliberate effort to make us realise the conditions of the present, and give them due preponderance over the suggestions of the past.

The one feature in the landscape, which, suggesting an intermediate stage, reminds us of the gradual nature of the transition from the original to the present sea-line, is Camber Castle. The name is supposed to have been Chamber Castle, or the castle between the two chambers or harbours of Rye and Winchelsea. It was built in the time of Henry VIII. upon a projecting tongue of land of low elevation, and upon the sea-line of his date. It is now about half-way between the two sea-lines of which we have been speaking.

We said above that the Rother had been the principal cause of the essential difference in character between Winchelsea and Rye, namely, that the latter is a living and the former a dead town. From the distance, as we are now observing them, this is the main apparent distinction; otherwise the similarity in site and general conditions is very striking. The outline of the promontories on which they stand is almost identical, rising gradually on the northern and terminating abruptly on the southern side. Each must have been at one period a peninsula; each is approached by a road which skirts the eastern side of the hill and gradually ascends, passes through a gateway, and is then lost to sight by a sudden turn to the right; in each the church was, or was meant to be, the apex of the pyramid. So much of similarity can be seen from our present position. When we come to examine each in detail we shall find some few further points of agreement, and more numerous points of difference. In both one striking feature is present. The main street running east and west leads to an abrupt descent on the eastern side of the hill, and on the very verge of the declivity turns suddenly to the left, forming the road of approach which we have been seeing from the windmill. The view looking eastward as you walk down the main street is very remarkable, and must have been more so when the expanse lying immediately below and stretching into the infinite distance was sea instead of marsh. But for the leading differences between the two, Rye is a city of unexplored antiquity, whereas the first stone of Winchelsea was laid in the thirteenth century. Rye was a timber city, and grew up fortuitously on an irregular plan; Winchelsea was a stone city, laid out regularly upon a plan of geometrical compartments. Rye Church is a conglomeration of schemes and styles, mostly of a rude vernacular character; Winchelsea Church is an almost ideal gem, of uniform character and of exquisitely studied detail.

But of all this there will be much more to say in connexion with a closer study of each city. So far we have had only a bird's-eye view of the Romney Marsh, and have got a general idea of its amphibious character. This is the principal note of the locality seen either from above or below. Indeed as we come down to its level, which is very level indeed, the impression of amphibiousness is by no means weakened. Not only do the more obvious and practical conditions lend themselves to this effect, such as the elaborate system of dams and deeply-cut drains filled with brackish water, the insular look of the little hamlets and village churches, the arrangements of rustic bridges and stepping-stones, set by the faithful of long-forgotten times, that they might worship dry-shod, safe from the water of flood-tides now ebbed for ever; but the more subtle effects are as those upon the sea. You see the storm gathering in the distance, and it sweeps over the equal ground self-contained, solid and detached, neither distorted nor delayed by any prominence; the wind blows steady and undiverted; and the countryman, who shows you a circuitous path to some distant object on the open plain, has some story to tell of former perils by sea. The farmers keep a few boats, and the retired sailors become farmers or farm-labourers, and the old houses far inland are specially and elaborately planned for hiding smugglers and smuggled goods. Moreover the sea, though from the dead level it is actually unseen, is constantly present to the imagination as a haunting influence, and to the senses as a bright horizon of reflected light; and the sea-shore is marked here and there by a low line of white-washed cottages and a flagstaff.

Next to amphibiousness, isolation is the most striking characteristic of the locality. Every one knows the celebrated subdivision of the world into Europe, Asia, Africa, America, and the Romney Marsh, and the sense of being lost seems to hang about the very air and to be breathed unconsciously into the soul. It is a reaction against this penetrating sensation rather than any dislike to the country which makes you constantly remind yourself that an hour's drive will at any time take you to the nearest railway-station and two hours to London. At least the inhabitants, though possibly capable of this calculation, seem as if they made little practical use of it. New Romney has the air of a Kentish village carried violently into a strange land, its links and associations snapped; and Lydd looks as if it were indebted to the loss of the *Northfleet* for any recognition whatever of an outer world.

On the level too we get now and again traces of the gradual change from sea to land, of which transition Camber Castle was the monument we saw from the height. Coming, for instance, on Old Romney, now some four miles distant from the sea, and reflecting that it was a Saxon port, that as a port it remained open until the Conquest, when New Romney, itself high and dry by some two miles at the present moment, was built, we look—not in vain—for traces of its original seafaring condition. Old Romney Church stands on a low, isolated hillock, obviously just clear of the flood-tide of antiquity; and a continuous succession of fields running seawards between parallel fences, and with a central depression, marks the channel which kept the port open centuries after the last high tide had ebbed. A few ruined churches to right and left, looking very weird and very desolate in a distance which from its bare monotony we cannot estimate, give us a sense of life ebbed as hopelessly as the sea.

Nevertheless, in spite of the equivocal aspects above noted, and apart from the treasures of art which this like almost every other province of England discloses when properly explored, the Marsh has a peculiar charm of its own. As you drive along a road bounded by deep cuttings

ON ROMNEY MARSH.

fringed with a deep-brown funereal reed, it is borne in upon you that the scene is as beautiful as it is strange. As you look over field upon field into distance upon distance, recognised solely by delicate atmospheric change, and see each willow a little greyer, and the tile-roof of each homestead a little less red, and each haystack a shade less golden than the nearer one, till all fades into a shadowy fringe in which individual objects are matters for conjecture, a sense of space and of mystery steals over you which might have inspired David Cox or De Wint; then further, as you watch remote objects and unconsciously guess at their relative distances, and a sense of motion in one or more of them gains upon you, and finally you become aware that they are ships in full sail in

OLD ROMNEY CHURCH.

the offing and on the same level as the trees and the haystacks and only a little more distant; then the sense of strangeness and the sense of amphibiousness rush together, and you feel as detached from the ordinary interests of the world and as amphibious as the oldest inhabitant.

It is just this kind of sentiment in landscape, this sense of personal identification with the physical conditions of the soil, which is the most penetrating, the most wholesome, and therefore the most permanent charm: it is this which has been and will be the motive of the truest art of external nature; and it proceeds neither from grandeur of scale nor ruggedness of outline nor from a vivid clearness of atmosphere nor from any special or exotic conditions whatever, but grows up in the simplicity and grave harmony of native scenes, and demands no energy and no effort, but only a little sensitiveness and a little sympathy.

II.

WINCHELSEA.

THE present aspect of Winchelsea is desolate and sad to the last degree. The melancholy impression it makes on us is partly strengthened, partly diminished, by some knowledge of its history. On the one hand, it is enhanced by the recognition of an almost unbroken succession of calamities from the date of its very earliest records; on the other, it loses so much of sadness as lies in the contrast of past prosperity with present ruin.

The causes of this continuous misfortune have been many and various—civil war, the doubly capricious enmity of the sea, the ambition of the founders of the new city, and foreign invasion. The effect of each of these agents towards the dreary result will be shown in a brief summary of the history of the town.

The site of Old Winchelsea lay some three miles south-east of the present town, and must have been built upon the extreme end of the tongue of land which formed the continuation of the Fairlight range of hills. Together with Rye it was the earliest supplement to the original Cinque Ports, and may therefore be considered to have enjoyed some celebrity at an early date. About 1236 the encroachments of the sea began to endanger its existence, and inundations of successively increasing severity followed at short intervals, until in 1288 the inhabitants—as many, or rather as few, of them as survived—were compelled to petition for a new site. The few only who survived; for not only had the population of Old Winchelsea been decimated by the inundations, but had further involved itself with an enemy little less ruthless than the sea. By siding with Simon de Montfort and clinging to his cause long after it had become hopeless, the men of Winchelsea had rendered themselves obnoxious to the higher powers, and fell victims to

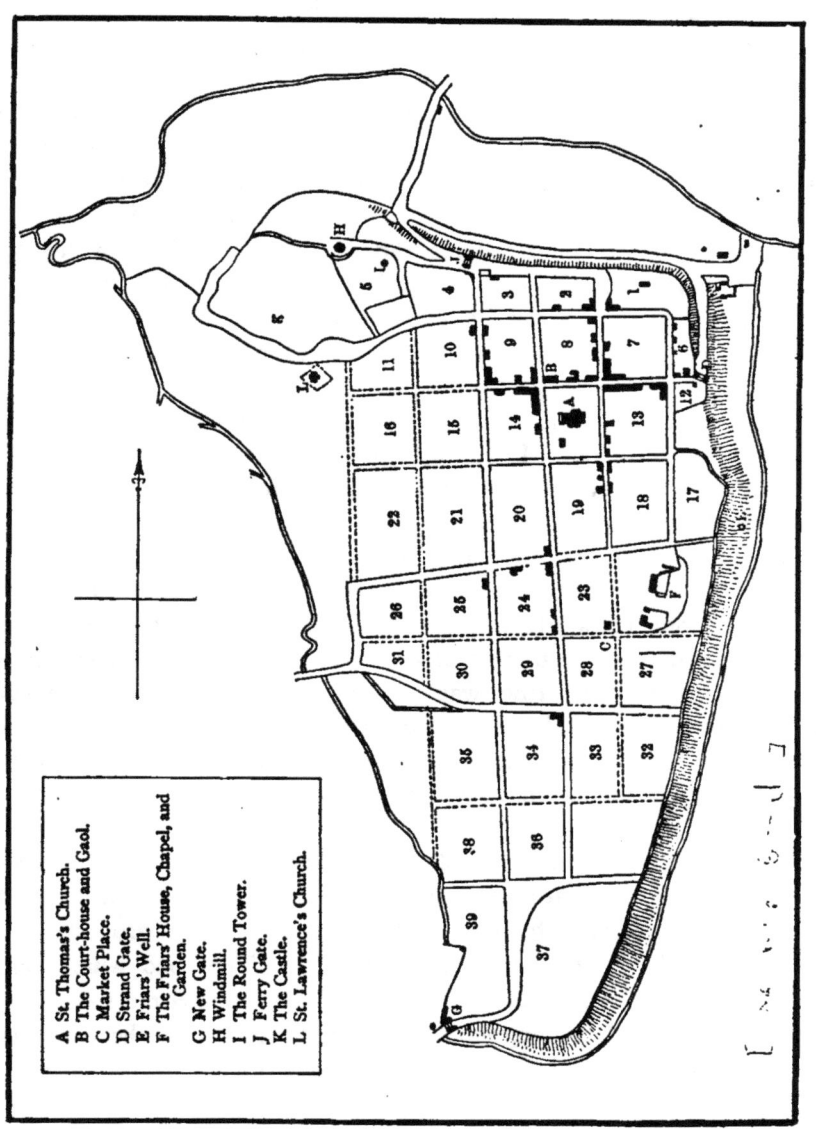

GROUND-PLAN OF WINCHELSEA, RESTORED.

such a vigorous and uncompromising treatment as was typical of the much-regretted middle ages, the direct efficiency of which cannot be too highly appreciated. That is to say, Prince Edward made all but a clean sweep of them. On the whole, though the men of those days were unquestionably inured to a certain asperity both in the physical and moral aspect of the universe, it cannot have been a very lively colony which left its habitations a permanent legacy to the fishes, and sought to transfer itself to the high and safe neighbouring promontory, 'the which was at that time a ground wher conies partily did resorte,' as Leland quaintly describes it. Thus did Neptune provide for his own flock at the expense of the rabbits; and if it is in any way conceivable that a sum of human life can be expressed in terms of fishes, probably Old Winchelsea has in point of liveliness had permanently the better of it.

All that authority could do to insure the prosperity of the new town was abundantly done; indeed overdone, as experience proved. Edward I. was a theorist on the subject of towns, and founded Winchelsea upon the model of the towns in France known as Villes-franches and Villes-neuves, names which note respectively their special municipal and geometrical conditions. By the latter, these towns were laid out in strict rectangles of equal size; one rectangle was made a market-place, another the site of a church or cathedral (in this aspect Montpazier is the most perfect example extant); by the former was granted every kind of privilege, such as independence of feudal lords, perfect freedom of movement, &c., which might induce persons to become citizens. This plan of provincial centralisation must unquestionably have had a tendency at that period to forward the civilisation of Europe.

The conditions of the site of New Winchelsea are on the whole similar to those of Rye, with one exception, namely, that on the west side the former is unprotected by the abrupt descent of the ground. The principal approaches were west and north-west. The road which skirts the eastern side of the promontory, and leads up to the Strand Gate, was no doubt the principal thoroughfare between the port and the town, and probably had to creep under the northern side of the high ground to give access to the adjoining country. The southern, eastern, and northern sides still retain all the appearance of having been washed by the sea, and undoubtedly at the period of its foundation the site of New Winchelsea must have been a peninsula. That this was the case is noted in a variety of ways. One of the gates, that which led to the port, is called the Strand Gate. Another, which must have stood just above the estuary which bounded the north side of the peninsula, is called, among other names, the Ferry Gate. Further, the west side of the town alone appeared to its founders to need artificial fortification, and this was obtained in the form of a deep moat, which may still be traced.

New Winchelsea then was founded on a regular geometrical system; but from the irregularity of the natural boundaries it varied considerably from the ideal rectangular form. The entire space included in the original

STRAND GATE, WINCHELSEA.

scheme amounted to some 150 acres, subdivided into plots varying from about one and a half to three acres, thirty-nine in all. One of these is the site of the church, another of the market-place. The remaining plots appear to have been very sparsely built upon in the best days of Winchelsea. As early as Henry V. the scheme appears to have been found to be too ambitious, as the Land Gate notes a contraction of the area of the town on the western side.

It was probably the ambitious character of the original scheme which made Winchelsea so easy and so constant a victim to foreign invasion. We read that the town was invaded, spoiled, and fired, and many of the inhabitants put to the sword by the French, in 1359; that a second invasion followed in 1377, which was however repelled by the bravery of the Abbot of Battle; that in 1380 it was taken by John de Vienne, and was again fired by the French in 1449. The superabundance of space in the plan, especially calamitous to a sea-port town, must have contributed not a little to make Winchelsea indefensible.

Finally, the fickle element which had importunately embraced Old Winchelsea, left its successor at a too respectful distance, indulging possibly in 'multitudinous laughter' at the fatal effects of so sinister a

LAND GATE, WINCHELSEA.

restitution. The poor town made some few struggles after a show of life, and actually won an encomium from Queen Elizabeth, who, as all the guide-books tell us, for the most part interpreting the royal compliment as a statistic, called it a 'little London.' But it was a feeble and hopeless effort, and since then the 'conies' might once more 'partly resorte' thither, for the entire population does not appear capable of mustering the sum of vitality requisite to shoot them.

Such is a brief summary of the actual history of the city; but for those who can find history apart from facts, to whom the colour and character of times and places have more of essential interest than matter-of-fact description or accurate chronology, Winchelsea must always have a deeper interest as the scene of Denis Duval's early history, the parish of the stately, humorous old Rector, as the abode of the squire—smuggler —highwayman, Joseph Weston, and the fatal De La Motte. To such readers this picture of a life of contraband and hard knocks and tender young loves and full-bottomed wigs in this perfect fragment, will be more vitally associated with the town and more real than all the records which research could bring to light. Who would not sooner identify the window

OLD HOUSE, WINCHELSEA.

from which little Agnes hung out her signals, 'a flower, for example, to indicate all was well, a cross-curtain, and so forth;' or the doorway from which Doctor Barnard walked out, erect and undaunted, to the yelling Protestant mob in front of those two 'foreign dissenting clergymen,' than the spot where Edward III. and the Black Prince landed after the battle with the Spaniards, or the eminence from which Queen Philippa's attendants watched it? Most of us probably find many a locality thus coloured for us with the genial light of fiction. In this manner Paris was for years to the present writer mainly the scene of the sufferings and death of a delightful homely heroine, under the good-natured imbecility of '*un bon enfant*,' her husband, and many a street-corner there still rouses a kind of sad curiosity in her interest; so too the iron chimney which surmounts Rouen Cathedral has to this day a weird fascination, as if it were a great monument of the crimes of the sinful, but alas! too captivating 'Emma' of Flaubert's masterpiece. So thoroughly does the highest fiction vindicate its right to local habitation, so truly can genius create more than history can renew.

To return to fact. The most important monument in Winchelsea is the church dedicated in honour of St. Thomas the Archbishop. It must have been commenced at the date of the foundation of the new town upon a very extensive plan. The extent of the site allotted, and the proportions of the completed parts, suggest a church of very great magnificence. But only the choir and its aisles remain: possibly they alone were ever actually completed. The transepts are in ruins, and there is no evidence that more than the foundations of the nave were ever executed. The remains of the church are among the richest in every element of fine design; and the perfect unity of the work, in which no variation of date is anywhere apparent, gives the fullest effect to its beauty. Of the illustrations, the exterior view in the frontispiece is taken from the north-east of the church and shows the choir with its two aisles. On the western angle of the northern aisle is placed the little squat spire, which is of a very casual but picturesque character. To the right are seen the remains of the southernmost bay of the original northern transept. The flying buttress at the north-eastern angle of the northern aisle was obviously an after-thought suggested by some settlement in the building. This is rendered certain by the fact that it is built against a smaller buttress, which exactly corresponds with that at the adjoining angle of the same aisle. That the settlement in question took place either during or immediately after the erection of the building is indicated by the character of the flying buttress, which is not perceptibly later than that which it strengthens, as well as by the continuity of the plinths of the basement. The enclosure of a square space of ground which resulted from this addition probably suggested a little lean-to erection, which may have been used as a sacristy. It may be pointed out that the east window is a restoration accomplished some years ago. Before that the window was filled with perpendicular tracery. The architect, prompted by a vulgar love for uniformity, removed this and replaced it by an ingenious conjecture of what the tracery filling this opening either was, or should have been.

TOMBS IN WINCHELSEA CHURCH.

The interior is composed of a choir and a north and south aisle, which terminate short of the extreme east. The arcade of grouped shafts, alternately of Purbeck marble, supporting arches of exquisitely designed mouldings, is as perfect in proportion as in detail. The sedilia of the choir must have been very refined and beautiful, their beauty being a matter of induction at the present moment, as they were restored some twenty years back and all the charm of workmanship lost. On the other hand, the sedilia of the south aisle are comparatively perfect; that is to say, they are partially mutilated and wholly unrestored. They form, with two magnificent tombs of Gervase and Stephen Alard—both admirals of the Cinque Ports—a continuous design along the entire south wall. Probably both monuments were executed about 1325, and the south aisle may have been wholly a chantry to the family of Alard. The interior view shows the aisle containing these tombs, with its sedilia, piscina and credence. No better example probably could be found in England of the manner in which interiors were completed in the middle ages, and the fact that all the several features are almost of the same date and that very little removed from the date of the main fabric, gives great additional value to the example. As regards the general arrangement, notice how boldly the different gablets cut the sill-line of the windows, standing out strongly against the light. Then again, how the same broad features are introduced into the several tombs and sedilia, and how, notwithstanding this, each has its own individuality in design. The scale of the present drawing necessarily makes it impossible for the reader to get more than a general impression of the character of the mouldings and carving, which are however marvellously perfect in refinement and beauty. All this work was of course gorgeously decorated, and some traces of colour may still be found here and there. Above the tombs, the windows, of quaint and elaborate tracery, are worked into a continuous design by the introduction into the intervals of small supplementary arches of a segmental character. The north aisle too is lined with a range of three monuments, occupants unknown, which have suffered so much from the building of a party-wall to screen off the vestry and from general neglect, that restoration is the only further deterioration which their state admits of. Externally it should be noted, that the tracery of the windows is set peculiarly near to the face of the walls, and looks well, although this arrangement is opposed to the spirit of later developments.

Further matters of interest with regard to the church are, that there is a vaulted crypt under the choir which was originally lighted, the windows being now closed up; that the foundations of the nave of the church are said to have remained until 1790, up to which date also remained a portion of a detached bell-tower towards the south-western extremity of the churchyard. Both are said to have been removed at the above-mentioned date to form Rye harbour, which was then building. But I can find no evidence whatever that the nave was ever completed.

We said above that the area of Winchelsea seemed to have been very sparsely built upon. Probably the allotments were intended to contain ample gardens; but even this limited scheme of occupation appears to have been only partially realised. The individual rectangular spaces are generally marked by the stone foundation, often showing just above the ground, sometimes rising to the height of some feet, and occasionally containing some fragment of mediæval detail: in a few cases a pointed doorway is found complete.

No entire domestic building remains. In many parts are vaulted cellars of very large dimensions, partly below and partly above ground; these may be taken to point to an extensive trade in French wines between Winchelsea and Boulogne. They are too innocently *en évidence* for purposes of smuggling, one would think; possibly however extensive cellarage was a feature of mediæval house-building, even where no special conditions called for it. The rooms above the cellars are usually reached by a small flight of steps from the street. The stonework appears most usually to have included the ground-floor, and above that may have been the timber construction covered with weather-tiling, which is characteristic of Kent and Sussex, and which no doubt dates from a far earlier period than is generally supposed. Evidence against this supposition is found in the remains of a house, of which an illustration is given on p. 19, which shows a mediæval buttress reaching a higher level than the termination of the ground-floor story, as well as in an appearance of old character in the masonry adjoining the chimney-stack. The latter is entirely of stone, as it well might have been even if the superstructure had been of timber and tiles. Between the church

Winchelsea. 23

and the Strand Gate is a block of houses of the kind we imagine to have been general. The timber-and-tile superstructure is not actually ancient like the stonework of the cellars and first floor, but has probably

COURT-HOUSE AND GAOL.

been renewed in the original character. We may well suppose that both manners of building were employed simultaneously, and that probably the more municipal and more monumental buildings were erected in the more permanent material. Some colour is given to this supposition by the fact

that the most pretentious of the existing fragments, the Court-house and Gaol, standing to the north-west of the church, is entirely of stone. This building is surmounted by a panelled stone chimney, of which an illustration is given. The capping of the chimney-stack has perished. The building itself is full of details pointing to its earlier uses. Thus there appears to have been an arcading along the ground-floor and a lean-to roof on two sides of the building and doorways, now closed, which probably led to the cellar; but the original design is lost past hope of recovery.

The Friary contains some interesting remains of the ancient chapel of the Virgin—a building of one span terminating in an apse. The

THE FRIARY.

choir-arch, which is the limit of the building westward, is very original in character. The triple shaft and capital is terminated by an abacus struck from one centre on plan, an arrangement by which the group is bound together; and the arch which it carries has a slightly 'horse-shoe' appearance. Whether it was actually built in this form, or whether it gained it by the settlement of the masonry, or whether the appearance is an optical illusion resulting from the stilting of the arch, must remain matter for conjecture. One feature characteristic of mediæval design

Winchelsea. 25

should be noted. The capitals supporting this arch are carefully and delicately moulded. A string of much bolder profile terminates the internal sill of the windows and returns round the triple shaft, to which it forms an anule. The contrast between the delicacy of the cap and the comparative coarseness of the string-course and the peculiar proportion between the two members of the grouped shaft caused by this subdivision, give a fortuitous and unstudied character to the design, and note the vigour and fearlessness with which the designers of the Middle Ages

NEW GATE, WINCHELSEA.

settled casual problems over which a modern architect might give himself hours of labour. Possibly the attempt to reproduce such effects under the essentially opposite conditions, both of mental habit and of executive method, which are characteristic of the present time, would convey an impression of studied carelessness, and consequently of affectation. This building differs very slightly in date, and very considerably in character, from St. Thomas's Church; which fact confirms the idea, suggested by the study of so many localities, of two distinct guilds of masons working simultaneously in one neighbourhood, but preserving the characteristics of their several styles intact. Probably the Franciscans, the founders of this church, had their own school of design and their own workmen.

It remains only to notice the three gateways, of which illustrations are given. On page 18 is the Land Gate—called also the 'Ferry Gate' —which, as we have seen, notes a reduced ambition in the scheme of the town. It contains no details of any interest except a shield, on which is carved the word 'Helde,' the name of the Mayor of Winchelsea *temp*. Henry V. when the gate was built.

To the extreme south is New Gate, on the road to Fairlight. This gate is nearly a mile distant from that last mentioned, and is at the present moment far removed from any remains of the town.

Returning through the streets of the ruined, or more probably unbuilt, southern portion of the town, we leave 'the Friars' on the right and pass St. Thomas's Church on the left, and turning to the right into what must always have been, and still is, the main street of Winchelsea, we get a magnificent view, over the marshes, of Rye, the sister acropolis, of which the grouping and colour are from this point very perfect; then we turn sharply to the left and come upon the Strand Gate, already illustrated, and note as we pass a doorhead adorned by a panel of delicate tracery; then descend, skirting the hill down to the probable site of the ancient port, and so quit Winchelsea for the scarcely more desolate Marsh.

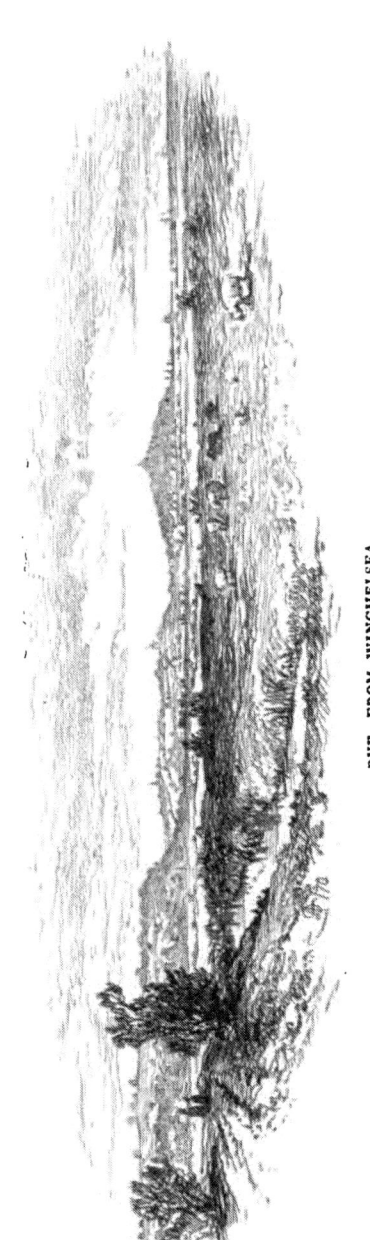

RYE, FROM WINCHELSEA.

III.

RYE.

TO make the most of any place which you visit for the first time you should reach it at sunset. At that hour the effects of landscape and cities are most mysterious and suggestive, and the mind too is impressed with a sense of vague imaginations, which become centred round the place you are reaching, and endow it with unlimited promise of interest and pleasure. Then again there is no fear of discounting the full revelations of daylight. When you have got rid of the discomfort and restlessness of travelling and have an hour to look about you, you can explore the new locality with a sense of perfect vacancy and irresponsibility, only modified not unpleasantly by the suspicion of a fear of losing your way, and can make a note of this object and that which seem likely to prove worthy of study by day. At this time more than any other it is possible to enjoy the feeling of being uprooted and placed in a fresh soil. The phenomena of the outer world have so much of indefiniteness and of a softened outline, that even in the most ordinary locality you may indulge in a temporary relief from the vulgar precision of everyday presentments, and may in the nineteenth century find a little interval in which the imagination may move uninjured by collision with vulgar realities. And when, as at Rye, the whole aspect and position of the place you have reached is a link with a far-off past, when at every street-corner some fragment at least raises suggestions of other days and gives promise of delightful study, then you feel a security in the vaguer pleasures which may be relied on to stand the test of daylight.

A very informal kind of branch-line takes you from Ashford to Rye across the bed of the Romney Marsh, of the character of which in passing you get a foretaste in a modified form, and brings you to a station on the north side of Rye; while Playden Hill, still having the appearance of the sea-cliff it formerly was, stands wooded and dark on your right hand. You alight on the beach of the original northern estuary and mount a steepish ascent, passing the position of the postern-gate, and getting in the twilight an indistinct vision of the old wall-line; and so

A TUDOR HOUSE.

TUDOR DOOR.

reach the main street, where is the principal inn, of which the primitive appearance gives promise at least of an immunity from modern æsthetics, which may compensate for deficiency in modern comforts. Wandering at random over the town in the evening, first of all the church comes on you suddenly at the end of a narrow street of old houses. After passing the church you come to a ruined keep, close to which a long flight of stone steps winds downwards to the level marsh on the south of Rye; and at the bottom of the steps is a small inn, the site of which, retired as it is and at the same time accessible, probably dates from the time when smuggling considerations were paramount in the choice of position. On this spot the sudden cessation of the lively, garrulous little town, the fall of the ground, the maritime-looking steps, a suspicion of tar and a dim vision of what may be masts, bring sea rather than land to the imagination as the occupant of the flat extent beyond: but the silence on a breezy evening, the lights in the distance unreflected, and a mass of dark shadow here and there, which seems to be the clump of trees round a neighbouring homestead, re-assert the conditions of the present and remove the sea to its actual limit two miles away. There are many old streets to explore, one of which, in its steep descent towards the quay, with two deserted old houses frowning story over story, promises a wealth of the picturesque. Then the main street again brings you to another eminence overlooking another ambiguous expanse, and it is time to return to the inn, with the prospect of turning the evening's notes into sterling architectural studies to-morrow morning.

The site of Rye must have been habitable from a very early geological period. Instead of emerging from the sea and gradually extending its limits, as did the sites of some of the other cities of the Marsh, it must have possessed at a remote age a far wider area than at present, and its history must have been one of gradual diminution up to the time when the sea left it. It is strange, therefore, that no records remain of Rye as an inhabited region till a comparatively late date—long subsequent to the earliest mention of Romney, for instance, whose supra-marine existence must have been comparatively very recent. The earliest mention found of Rye is to the effect that Edward the Confessor gave it with Winchelsea to the Abbey of Fécamp in Normandy, at the same time bestowing on the monks of that abbey such rights of visitation and supervision as would enable them to collect their revenues. The revenues of the town continued thus alienated until the time of Henry III., who, finding that the right of entry into so accessible a town was one eminently capable of abuse, as giving the French a ready means of *espionage* in time of war, resumed the royal rights over the port, and gave in exchange the manors of Chilcenham and Scloutr in Gloucestershire, and the manor of Naveneby in Lincolnshire. Rye, as we have seen, was with Winchelsea added to the Cinque Ports before the end of the twelfth century, at least a century after the charters of the Cinque Ports were originally granted.

It is somewhat difficult to determine at what period Rye ceased to be an island. It may be inferred that the Marsh to the north was partially enclosed as early as Edward III.'s time, as it then appeared to be necessary to give it artificial defence upon the land side. The other sides were sufficiently protected from all enemies but the sea by the abruptness of the ground. The sea, however, appears to have reduced the limits of the town very considerably, especially on the south-eastern

THE LAND GATE, RYE.

and eastern side; 'where,' as Leland says, 'hath been washed away some streets, the Baddings Gate and wall leading therefrom to the Land Gate.'

At the present time the principal road of approach to Rye, after passing through the last-mentioned gate, begins to bear towards the right, and on reaching the higher ground makes an abrupt and almost rectangular turn still in the same direction. This arrangement is due to the curtailment of the eastern cliff; for this road of approach continued formerly in a

RYE AND THE ROTHER.

direct line to the extreme southern limit of Rye, where must have been the Baddings Gate alluded to above. There is also evidence in the recorded position of rocks, fragments of the perished cliff, to some distance south of the present town, that the island at least, if not the town, formerly extended far in this direction.

Though the town has at the present time here and there overstepped its artificial boundaries, they are still sufficiently apparent. Making its circuit from the Land Gate in a westerly direction, you can trace the old wall of Edward III., with here and there an inconsiderable interval, as far as the remains of the West Gate. It does not indeed retain its integrity as a fortified wall, nor is it easily accessible. Here it is the retaining wall of a garden, there the lower story of a dwelling-house, or of one or other of those picturesque amphibious buildings which mark an English port. You identify its position at other points by a few fragments of weather-worn stone incorporated in a brick wall, and discerned through a vista of sculleries and backyards; but you never lose sight of it long enough to feel any doubt of its precise position. With the Strand Gate, of which fragments still remain, the cliff begins and the artificial fortification ceases. The maritime buildings cling to the cliff to some small distance southward, and then leave it free to mark the limit of the town on the south and south-eastern side, until the Land Gate from which we started is reached again.

One of the most characteristic views of Rye is that of the Western Cliff, at the point where it begins to free itself from the surrounding buildings just south of the Strand Gate. You look towards the town across the Rother, over one of those effective foregrounds of river and all the picturesque paraphernalia of shipping—the broken cliff with its rude shapes of rock overgrown and softened by the rich vegetation of vines, mallow, long grasses and docks, here and there strengthened and buttressed by rude masonry, topped by vernacular buildings with quaint gables and chimney-stacks, and a wooden summer-house or two, the look-out probably of some retired skipper, while the whole promontory terminates in the level waste marsh stretching unbroken into infinite distance. Rye has, in this general aspect, at least the strangeness of a foreign town, and its individual remains are certainly not less interesting.

Before considering each of them separately, it only remains to record very briefly the few historical facts in the history of the town which possess any general interest.

Rye, like Winchelsea, appears to have been exposed to frequent attacks from the French, the most memorable of which was in 1378, and is described by Stow in the following terms of very dubious import :—

'They within five hours brought it wholly into ashes, with the church that then was there of a wonderful beauty, conveying away four of the richest of that town prisoners, and slaying sixty-six, left not above eight in the towne. Forty-two hogsheads of wine they carried thence to their ships with the rest of their booty, and left the towne desolate.'

That this account, so far as it is intelligible, is probably greatly exaggerated, is indicated by the fact, that in 1448 Rye was deemed worthy of another attack by the French, when it was again captured. In the time of Henry VII. it lost its merchant fleet, and is said never since then to have recovered its ancient mercantile prosperity. The reports of antiquaries, however, are apt to produce a somewhat dismal impression on the mind; possibly, among others, for the two following reasons: that calamities, being distinct, several events, are more apt to survive in a fragmentary record than the less definite features of gradual progress; and because the historian or antiquary of former days, lacking that invaluable safety-valve of sensationalism, the three-volume novel, which was still in the future, was naturally led to colour somewhat highly the events he had to record. So far as the present aspect of Rye affords a criterion of the truth of these accounts, I should be disposed to modify them considerably. At any rate, Rye is at this moment, notwithstanding the increased difficulty of access from the sea, a sufficiently prosperous little town, with all the blessings of a market-place, a member of parliament, and quarter-sessions.

After the church, which is reserved for the next chapter, the most notable building in Rye is the Ypres Tower, which stands at the south-eastern corner of Rye, at the head of the flight of stone steps leading down to the level ground which was formerly the beach. The only portion of the original Ypres Tower which appears in the illustration is the round angle-tower in the distance, the square battlemented building in front of it being a modern addition. Ypres Tower is a square building with a round turret at each angle. In one of these is a circular staircase leading to the different floors. It was built by William de Ypres, Earl of Kent, in the reign of Stephen, and continued to be a tower of observation and defence, probably until the latter part of the fifteenth century, when it was converted into a gaol; adjoining it was formerly

STAIRS LEADING TO THE YPRES TOWER.

the Gun-garden Gate. Besides its position, there is no very special interest attaching to this tower, except in the admirable architectural expression in the doorways and windows of the uses to which it is at present applied. These fittings, though they possess little detail by which their date may be assigned, appear to belong to the fifteenth century. It is well worthy of note how, by a liberal use of material, a thoroughly workmanlike appreciation of the conditions of their practical use, and a certain *naïveté* and simple ingenuity of method, they attain to a considerable degree of æsthetic merit. Notice, for instance, the strong *grille* with its wide iron margin, the bolts of massive iron, with just a touch of ornamentation which the workman could not help adding, because workmen were artists in those days, with the hasp or perpendicular bolt to drop behind it and keep it from being unshot from the inside. Then see how the lock is secured to the door by a huge oaken stile, riveted to the door by bands of iron which crowbars could scarcely move. Then observe the ready ingenuity with which the special conditions of each several doorway are turned to account. At the top of the page of illustrations, on the right-hand side, we see how the position of the door opposite to a wall of solid masonry has suggested the expedient of forming a strong buttress against the door, when shut, by dropping a powerful iron bar hung to the masonry into a loop fixed in the head of the door. On the bottom of the page to the left is a door communicating with one of the corner chambers of the tower, for which room has been made by forming a recess in the wall with half of a segmental circle above it. In the drawing at the bottom of the page on the right you see how there has been a difficulty in getting a receiver for the locks and bolts of the door, which difficulty has been surmounted by securing a huge oaken log to the masonry by means of strong iron hooks. The readiness and informality of such expedients, the sense of the vigorous action of unfettered intelligence in the simple and natural resolution of casual problems, possess so great a charm that it is no wonder that the styles of the Middle Ages have an abundant following. Again, the elasticity of the Gothic styles, which allowed each practical feature to gain its appropriate expression, has perhaps been scarcely adequately appreciated by the most devoted practical exponents of Gothic. As an example of this characteristic I have placed together on p. 28 two domestic doorways of about the same period. The

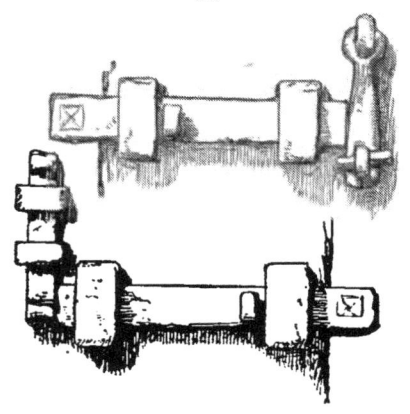

DOORWAYS IN YPRES TOWER.

homely and refined expression of these is as apparent as the gaunt, forbidding character of those from the Ypres Tower, and is attained with the same unconscious ease. Somehow or other, unconsciousness and elasticity are of all others the elements of effect which seem most foreign

POCOCK'S SCHOOL.

to the contemporary mind, and which are most conspicuously absent from the modern school of domestic Gothic, under the auspices of which prisons are too apt to look like houses and houses like prisons, and both and all to look affected to an extreme degree.

A very interesting specimen of the more formal and studied character of design introduced by the Renaissance is Pocock's School. It is specially worthy of notice as being a remarkably early specimen of the pilaster treatment, having been erected in 1636, as possessing a certain vernacular and maritime character, and as showing signs of the transition by which

the later gradually gained upon and eclipsed the earlier style. In the doors, for example, we have the old vernacular Gothic doorway, with a semicircular head and a modification of moulding. In the chimney opening on the first floor the two elements are almost equally balanced, and the mullioned and transomed windows are a survival of the earlier style. On the other hand, the general renaissance character is very strongly pronounced in the design as a whole, which is perfectly formal and symmetrical. The architect, however, has evidently been greatly puzzled by the novel conditions. Notice, for example, what an embarrassment the cornice has been to him, and how he has been obliged to cover it with a tile-roof of considerable expanse. Then observe the clumsy proportion of the pedestals of the pilasters, the projection of which detracts appreciably from the width of the street, and how the bases of the pilasters only just stop short of the glass of the lower windows, which they divide very awkwardly in the centre. The astounding proportion of the several members suggests a most diverting ignorance of the laws of the orders, and looks as if the architect had got his knowledge, such as it was, in some extremely indirect manner. On the other hand, its very quaintness and irregularity give it a special interest, even if we did not remember that it is illustrious as the scene of Denis Duval's school-days. As an instance of the extreme elaboration which the style thus introduced ultimately reached, we give in conclusion a Georgian doorway to a doctor's house, near the top of Mermaid Street; with regard to which we may note, that notwithstanding its extreme intricacy of detail and classicality of expression it still retains the note of the vernacular character, showing that the style had really taken root in out-of-the-way places.

IV.

RYE CHURCH.

THERE is a period in the history of all reforms, however necessary they may have been, when their very success makes it impossible for them to retain the enthusiasm with which they were inaugurated, when the new idea has passed into the category of commonplaces and has lost its power of stimulating the imagination, which is then apt to revert with something of tenderness to the supplanted heresy or vice. The latter has acquired all the attractive force that centres round objects which have associations in the past and no prospective rights in the future; as being in a minority, it enlists the favour of the chivalrous, and as a rarity the fancy of the connoisseur.

It is earnestly to be hoped that even the twentieth century of our era may possess here and there an unrestored church. The restoring persuasion has had it all its own way for some years past. Holocausts of pews galleries and tablets have been offered up to the new idea. Old-new churches, with spick-and-span correct fittings, are plenty as blackberries; and we are almost prepared to confess to a sneaking tenderness for the high, drowsy-looking pews, gloomy aisle-galleries, and the Commandments in the vulgar tongue; even to a mild tolerance for the three-decker. Hogarth's picture of the afternoon service, with all its ugliness, brings with it a redeeming whiff of a past atmosphere; and in a busy and earnest age, when every one will have us be logical and common-sense and practical, when progressive ideas are about our path and about our bed and reach us four times a-day hot from the brain of the public instructor, it is a momentary relief to breathe the drowsy atmosphere which hangs about a time before earnestness was invented; when the parson delivered perfunctorily a sand-glass full of sound and dull theology, and the congregation slept deliberately and woke up with a quite illogical sense of edification; when people were generally quiet and frequently dull, and had no sense whatever of the deep meaning and huge responsibility of living; but did nevertheless here and there many things which our earnest contemporaries are glad enough humbly to imitate at a very considerable distance.

We would earnestly plead before Sir John Lubbock's Commissioners of Antiquities* that a few old churches, with the eighteenth-century function intact and a parson to preach in the same spirit, should be retained here and there in accessible places throughout the country, and more especially within easy reach of the metropolis. So, when Mr. Leslie Stephen and the Positivists have stripped us of our last anomaly, and we have been made perfect in the light of the coming age, and have learnt to exult in limiting our thoughts and hopes for the future of ourselves and our friends to the innocuous residuum of cremation, which we shall high-mindedly utilise in the cabbage-garden, we may occasionally on a Sunday, if Sundays then there be, escape from the overpowering blessings of our high calling to consistency and logic, and doze for a placid hour in an atmosphere of exploded art and annihilated theology.

Possibly however this view of the matter may seem to the reader to be fanciful. Even then he will scarcely fail to appreciate a whole range of considerations in favour of the strictest conservatism in questions of restoration. An unrestored church has about it all the charm of infinite possibilities unrealized. All that the past has left it is there. All that the future can do for it may be created by the imagination. It is not only in questions of restoration that we hesitate to discount the possible for the actual. It is an intelligent and harmless amusement, both for professional and amateur architects, to effect restorations of the most thorough and complete kind on the tablets of the brain or even upon paper. I know of few more interesting pastimes than for a number of architects, archæologists and admiring *dilettanti*, to visit an ancient building, and there to enter upon a tournament of imaginary restorations, provided only that there be an absolute predetermination on the part of its owners and guardians to carry out no single one of the suggestions. Otherwise the game is played with too heavy a stake to be

* When this was written the Bill for the appointment of such a Commission was under consideration, and the writer was rash enough to anticipate that a Conservative Government would extend to our most valuable monuments some portion of that tenderness which it is supposed to show for abuses.

an innocent amusement, with a property to wit of future ages, of quite immeasurable value. Seriously however, admitting as one must that churches may and must be adapted to modern uses, I maintain without reserve and without exception that the obliteration of any ancient feature whatever in an old church is unnecessary and unjustifiable, and that in the great majority of instances restoration should be merely repair. An old church, as for example that which we are about to consider, is frequently not one, but many churches in one. It is possible to trace in it a whole series of rebuildings and to estimate with accuracy the period and the extent of each. A modern love of uniformity often leads to the obliteration of every style but one, and thereby sacrifices a genuine and

RYE CHURCH.

many-sided historical treasure for the very remote chance of attaining a superior artistic result; remote, because in an age characterised by fluctuations of taste and poverty of design, it needs sublime self-confidence to suppose that one's productions will bear the light of a more æsthetic future generation. At any rate—and this is more directly to our present purpose—Rye Church is not restored. You feel this almost before you catch sight of it and gain the full relief of being saved from a bathos which would have the effect of a phrase of slang in 'Paradise Lost.'

Of external history in connexion with Rye Church not much is to be found. The historians speak of another earlier church on a site somewhat south of that of the existing building. The antiquary, with characteristic temerity, states that it was a timber church: because forsooth there have been such things as timber churches, and because there was timber to be had within reach. Having examined the very small amount of evidence which exists on the subject, I am disposed to think that the present building incorporates all that there ever was of church in Rye. What details remain are as early as any one would expect to find, and there is abundant proof throughout the length and breadth of the country that a change of site was very unusual in the Middle Ages. Moreover, the whole theory may have originated in the misunderstanding of some ancient record to the effect that the old church was destroyed and a new church built.

Internal evidence shows that a Romanesque Church was commenced upon this site. Probably the building had not progressed far before the 'transitional' character, in which the church is mainly built, crept into the style. The thirteenth and fourteenth centuries contributed respectively a range of triforiated windows on the side of the northern aisle, and a flying buttress to the east of the church. Towards the end of the fifteenth and in the beginning of the sixteenth century the church was partly added to and partly altered in the prevailing style of that date. The additions were mainly the clerestory of the nave, the larger traceried windows, the pulpit and the aisle-screens. With some of the alterations we shall have to do presently.

The general condition of the church is one which is specially valuable to archæologists, for the characteristic features of each style are sufficiently evident; no effort towards congruity appears ever to have been made until the latest modification, and this, as we shall see, has for our instruction been left incomplete. Some features suggesting former conditions of the structure are apparent in the illustration. For example, the remains of a round-arched doorway in the south transept are visible in the external view; in the internal view can be seen the corbels which mark the pitch of earlier roofs.

Before proceeding to illustrate the characteristic examples of rebuilding which occur in this church, it may perhaps not be superfluous to say a few words about the spirit in which the builders of the Middle Ages dealt with the monuments of their predecessors, and of the methods which they employed. This spirit was, with a very few exceptions, one of supreme contempt. It is the necessary penalty which men pay for an exclusive training in one school of art, that they should be blind to the merits of all others. On the other hand, the establishment of a universal standard of taste has almost invariably been the condition under which the greatest works of art have been produced; for under such conditions only can the full force of the mind be devoted to the production of actual work. In our own day, for the first time in the world's history, artists are called upon to create a style; and even when this irrational demand is put aside, the necessity of choice between a number of styles of nearly equal merit and adaptability, and the sense of isolation which each little section of artists must necessarily feel, detract greatly from the force which is available for design. A master-builder, then, of one of the later periods dealing with earlier work had no thought but by the readiest means to produce an *ensemble* in the established manner of his own time. Some few modifications of this exclusive spirit are here and there apparent. Some examples show for instance that the builders of one of the later periods have had so much respect for a Romanesque doorway as to incorporate it into a newly built aisle. Occasionally, as for example in Westminster Abbey, in making addition to an old building, the original design has been adhered to but for the modification of some minor details. But it is far more usual to come upon evidence that the earlier work was ruthlessly sacrificed and the ornamental details used in the heart of the new walls. I said above that a change of site was unusual in old churches. This is constantly indicated by the presence on the same spot and in the same structure of fragmentary details of every period. The walls of many churches which appear as uniform monuments of one of the later styles, are perfect museums of remains of work in the earlier styles. In removing a modern doorway from a sixteenth-century church, I have come upon fragments of Romanesque work of which no trace whatever was apparent in any part of the structure; and lately, in the destruction of a cubical church of the eighteenth century, I collected and classified fragments which would have illustrated a glossary of the Gothic styles without a flaw.

A slightly less contemptuous way of treating ancestral work was merely to build it up. For example, the doorway in the south transept of Rye Church alluded to above was simply built into the flat wall, and a coat of rough-cast to conceal the whole was either given or at least intended. But the most interesting phase of rebuilding is that of which two capital examples occur in this church; that, namely, by which a later character was given to the existing earlier work. Of this practice too there were various methods. One was to draw a section of mouldings which could be included in and cut out of the bulk of the existing work, and simply to chisel the new forms out of the old. This was

RYE CHURCH, LOOKING EAST.

the method pursued in the arcade of the north chancel aisle. Of the two sketches at the top of page 44, that on the left shows the detail of the original arcade, of the period of the transition between Romanesque and First Pointed work; on the right is another bay, in which the alteration has been partially carried out. The capital and the mouldings below and to a short distance above it have undergone the change. The mason was in this instance working upwards stone by stone, and has stopped, and there is the evidence of his method of handiwork to this day. Some of the other arches have been completely remodelled. The chancel arch has been modified in a similar manner, but as the work was in this case completed, the evidence of the change is not so direct. The reader will see, by carefully examining the interior view of the church, that the nave arch on the left belongs to the transitional period mentioned above. He will also perceive that the arch-mouldings are set very far back upon the abacus of the capital, by which an exceedingly clumsy appearance is given to the arch. This latter characteristic, as well as the same general proportions, is present in the chancel arch, and proves it to have been originally of the same date, which is further confirmed by the great crudity of the mouldings of the capital, the mason having had to be content with the best effect he could get out of the original stone. These points will be more easily seen in the accompanying marginal sketch, of which the proportions are more correctly given than in the general view of the interior.

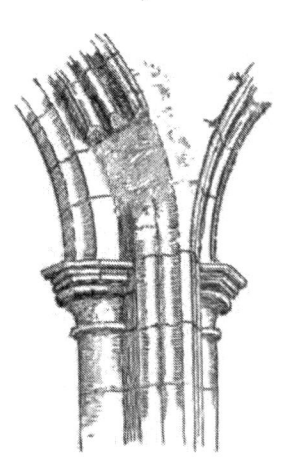

Another method of rebuilding was as follows. The new design was executed stone by stone upon the ground, and as each stone was completed its place was cut for it in the position which it was to occupy in the existing work and it was fixed therein. This rebuilding was often made from top to bottom; the entire facing of the work was new and of new material, and the original work remained only as a core to the new. The best-known and most readily intelligible example of this method is at St. Alban's Abbey, where again the work has been suspended and left incomplete; and another good example is Winchester Cathedral, of which the nave was rebuilt from the Romanesque to the Perpendicular style by William of Wykeham. The two easternmost arches, probably because they were intended to be filled up by monuments, remain partially unchanged.

Before quitting Rye Church we may remark especially the late pulpit, of which the linen-pattern panels and little buttresses are very characteristic and good, and the very simple and beautiful screen between the north aisle and the transept. These screens were an integral part of the design of a mediæval church, and their artistic value, as giving a mystery to all the richness and beauty behind them, is quite inestimable, but such as a generation which hankers after huge sheets of plate-glass for its windows will be slow to appreciate. Romney Marsh, owing no doubt to its isolation from advanced ideas, possesses an unusual amount of such features, which, in regions of greater intelligence, have been so generally sacrificed to the refined and interesting zeal of Protestantism.

Such considerations as the above naturally lead us to reflect on the

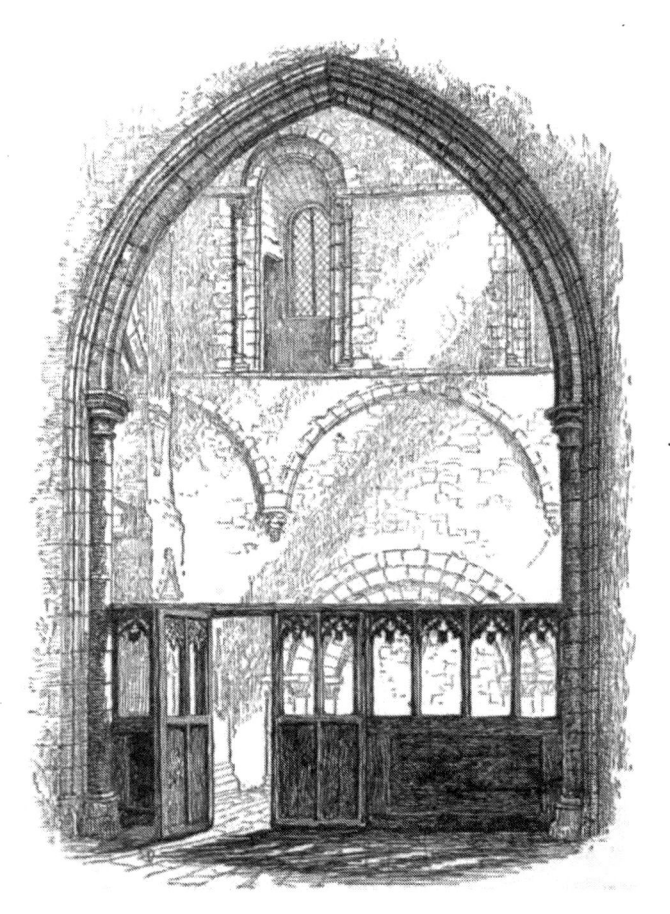

NORTH TRANSEPT, RYE CHURCH.

wide difference between the artistic ideal of the past and of the present. Features which were an essential and integral part of the effect aimed at in the middle ages have been completely eliminated from our modern practice as being either superfluous or detrimental; while the popular judgment, though founded upon a precedent of mutilated remains rather than of complete works of art, is as self-confident as even an uninterrupted tradition could make it. Few only of the critics of a modern ecclesiastical building finished up to the standard of the present day fully realise how incomplete an aspect it would present to the eyes of a mediæval artist, to whom it would be little more than the ground-work of a great artistic result. Decorations, which according to our present ideas are matters of exceptional, possibly of objectionable, luxury, were, in the intentions at least of the founders of the style we try to reproduce, absolute matters of course. To contentedly complete a church so that it shall represent one fresh from the mutilation of Protestant zeal is only a shade less absurd than to erect a ruined castle; and it is probably due to this misconception that so many spurious methods of veiling the obvious incompleteness have been arrived at. It is undoubtedly true that, owing to some essential changes in the conditions under which churches are now built, the full development of mediæval design in all its aspects is impossible; nevertheless it is only by a due comprehension of the full meaning of an artistic precedent in all its entirety that it can be profitably followed; and a modern designer who kept before his imagination the complete and perfect ideal would probably make a very different use of his limited opportunities to one who recognised only the more permanent and constructional conditions. The essential life and colour of mediæval art is unquestionably more apparent in the less monumental features, which having by comparison a purely expressional character, are left to impress the imagination unhampered by any utilitarian restraints. But space prevents me from entering more fully into the very wide question of the proper use to be made of mediæval examples. Some few remains out of the rich museum which Rye presents are still to be noticed.

From the main street of Rye a lane descends suddenly towards the low ground on the north. Half-way down this is an old Augustinian Priory, which has been turned into a warehouse for wool. The north side of the building, but for the suspicion here and there of a mediæval detail, has been converted into such an appearance as its present uses suggest; but the south presents one of those picturesque effects which in most minds are associated exclusively with foreign travel. A range of three traceried windows, to the sills of which the present level of the ground almost reaches, overgrown with vine, which finds the Gothic tracery an excellent trellis, forms the background of a pretty minute garden, full, when I saw it, of zinias, and marigolds, and other bright autumn flowers; the *ensemble* producing one of those charming effects of the picturesque which it would perhaps be barbarous to try to analyse. Perhaps the contrast of the present and the past life, and of the uses which the same feature serves in each, has much to do with this. Only

AUGUSTINIAN PRIORY, RYE.

the later use should be a simple one, chosen spontaneously and without intention of the picturesque, or the poetry disappears, as it does inevitably when the ruin is *encadré* by a trim flower-garden, through the fatal affection of some accomplished owner and connoisseur. To leave the picturesque for the architectural, the tracery of the windows, of which an enlarged drawing is given, presents an unusual and rather awkward character of late flowing work. The bases of the mullions, which are dropped and continued along the jamb-mouldings, are curious; especially because the junction of the two levels of base-moulding suggests the solution of the little casual problem by the ingenuity of the mason, its method being one which could never have been expressed on a drawing.

The remaining illustration shows a view up Mermaid Street, which, both from its steepness and the old houses it contains, is the most picturesque street of Rye. Some distance up the street on the left are two

TRACERIED WINDOW.

dignified old houses with overhanging roofs. To the right, in the foreground of this illustration, are the remains of the old West Gate, with the Cinque-port arms remaining. The other side of the gate has entirely disappeared, but its position and plan are probably indicated by the contour of the building on the left.

It is only fair to Rye that, in quitting it, we should recognise how very partial our researches there have been. Characteristic examples only have been selected from a vast storehouse of mediæval remains, which it would take a section of a lifetime to exhaust. But it is not so much its wealth of monuments as the special colour, character, and suggestiveness of the whole town which remain upon the memory; and it is some hint of this which we would gladly have conveyed to our readers.

MERMAID STREET, RYE.

V.

THE ROMNEY MARSH, THE ROMNEYS, AND LYDD.

A VERY wide tract of country, rich enough in monuments of antiquity, remains to be briefly dismissed in this chapter It would have been a very interesting task to have made some effort to trace the geological history of the Marsh; to have decided about when and in what order the various points emerged from the sea-level; to have sketched the various stages of the transition from sea to dry land, and to have realised the region, first, as a shallow sea with here and there a group of foaming breakers, then with one or more barren ridges of sand emerging at low water, later, as an archipelago of numerous sandy islands which the strong, clinging grass was binding together and consolidating, and slowly but surely converting into habitable soil; to have recorded who first and for what causes of feud or famine left the solid earth to try their fate upon the new birth of the ocean; to which of the existing towns or villages they gave a name, and what that name intended; to have traced the slow change from the group of habitable islands to the Marsh, with its wide pools of sea-water which deepened and shallowed with the flow and ebb of the tide; to have noted the stages of gradual transition from the occasional and intermittent communication between partially isolated village and village to the continuous and safe intercourse, in which stepping-stones only were the symbol of past dissociation, together with all the social changes which such a gradual fusion inaugurated; then to have recorded the full history of the means by which the dwellers on the Marsh made complete the work which nature had carried so far, and the occasions on which the sea, expelled by the spade, reasserted itself by still running back; to have noted how combination against an impersonal enemy consolidated the commonalty less sanguinarily but not less effectually than war; and to have ascertained how far exactly the proverbial conceit and exclusiveness of the people of the Marsh resulted from the consciousness of having expelled so formidable an invader. So much the present aspect of the tract of country implies of unwritten history—unwritten except in such record as each of us can read for himself with his eyes and his understanding; and better so, for with a sense of conflicting theories, unsupported conjectures, and of the general temerity with which, in such matters, an historical superstructure has frequently been founded on an absence of fact, it is certainly easier and perhaps not less instructive for us to limit our knowledge to such things as must have been. Here and there indeed, just as ethnologists see the nascent civilisation of the past in the savagery of the present, we may see one or more of the transitionary processes in actual operation. Near Lydd many miles of sea-beach have still to be worked into arable soil, and the sea is still pushed back year by year at a steady pace. Of a later period certainly, when the Marsh was permanently recovered and inhabited, many facts of interest are recorded both geological and political; but of all this very little need concern us at present. Those who care for detailed accounts of such matters may find endless discussion as to the point on the Marsh of the landing of Julius Cæsar; as to the meaning of the word Romney; and much so-called history founded on a conjectural derivation. The account of a Royal Commission sent by Henry III. to inquire into matters concerning the draining and embanking of the Marsh is less apocryphal; so also is the account of the diversion of the course of the Rother, which formerly debouched between Romney and Lydd, by the same storm which we have elsewhere commemorated as having given the *coup de grâce* to old Winchelsea.

Old Romney, whether or not it be considered the first point of emergence, has at least claims to precedence among the few places about which we shall have something to say. At present it consists of a little church which was illustrated before, and a few houses and cottages of little antiquity and no interest. The church is mainly of the fourteenth century, and is pewed and lime-whited after the taste of our great-grandfathers; but a small portion of the east wall, composed of smaller stones than the rest of the fabric, looks like a remnant of a much older building, probably of Saxon date; and in the tower, leading to the belfry, is a primitive staircase which may be as early as the thirteenth century. Then a deserted chancel-aisle contains crumbling remains of the screens of delicately carved wood-work, such as an age of universal art produced and an age of restoration usually destroys. Altogether Old Romney, possibly the metropolis of the Marsh, is in a dismal state of senility and decay.

Old Romney is said to have *dropped* downwards with the retiring sea-line till a fresh rallying-point was found in New Romney, which it is said was once connected with the former by a continuous line of houses. At any rate, New Romney must have been founded about the time of the Conquest, if we may judge from the date of the fine Norman tower of its only remaining church. Formerly it had five churches, of which some fragments may be seen incorporated in an artificial ruin, which some local *dilettante*, inspired by the genius of the place, has made for his habitation.

The general aspect of the village is, but for exceptional sleepiness, not widely different from that of a hundred villages of the southern counties, and, but for the dry channel which runs past it from Old Romney seawards, scarcely a trace of its former sea-faring condition remains; but evidence both of former prosperity and of former smuggling is to be found abundantly. In the New Inn is an old panelled room of about the time of James I., very quaint and characteristic and very elaborate, as is usual with features of that date, and a whole wing of the house with separate staircases and an infinity of stowage-room gives us an insight into the 'fair trade' which was the traditional profession of the men of the Marsh; a profession to which they still incline to revert, unless the tiny hamlets of low white cottages with their typical flagstaff, which may be detected here and there on the sea-line, are the abodes of sinecurists. Formerly even the aisles and chapels of the Marsh churches were pressed into the service of contraband, and no doubt the chauntry of many a noble and illustrious fair-trader was haunted by a flavour of smuggled brandy, more appropriate by far, more familiar, and doubtless more grateful to the occupant of the tomb, than the incense for which the more orthodox part of him had compounded.

But to leave matters of special local interest. The same inn, which has been added to and refitted at various times, contains one feature of no very exceptional character or importance, of which we may well say a few words. The illustration given over-leaf represents a dining-room cupboard, made not much later than the middle of the last century, and full of the character of that date. The shelves are carved to a charming shape, having a projection in the middle to carry the decanter, while the wine-glasses are ranged on either side. The whole is somewhat elaborate in design with its pilasters and keystone and returned cornices and rich mouldings, but notwithstanding that it is the focus of ornament in a room otherwise plainly finished with

CUPBOARD, NEW INN, NEW ROMNEY.

large panels, it is all shut in when not in actual use by a glazed door, through which the mouldings and rich decorations and sparkling glasses could be dimly discerned, as the altar-hangings and flowery vestments of the priests through the screen of a mediæval chapel. In this case the decorations are lost, if indeed they were ever completed; but since the present sketch was made I had the good fortune to find in a house of the same date, in another part of Kent, such another cupboard, with the original decorations as fresh as the day they were completed. In this case it may be observed that the door is unglazed, and the ornamentations therefore still less conspicuous. The pilasters and cornice and edges of the shelves are decorated in gold and red; the gold laid over red in all cases to give it additional richness. In the semi-dome at the top is a painting of Neptune driving his team of sea-horses. The inner side of the door and the plain surfaces of the cupboard are marbled in a very conventional manner, of which the aim was obviously to produce a pleasant broken effect of harmonious colour rather than to imitate another material. The rest of the room is plainly but beautifully finished, and it as well as all the rest of the house is unmutilated and unrestored—a complete monument of the past.

Not many such are to be found in England now; possibly because there are not many owners who repeat the best characteristics of an age more congenial to art; who, without any consciousness of enlightenment or taste, and without ambition of advancement or change, are content to live as their ancestors lived, and who, by a quiet, undiscursive communion with external nature, have acquired a natural, unconscious love for and contentment in beautiful things, apart from the restless phases of connoisseurship and fashion. Such was the life of those with whom this simple, quaint and refined domestic art of the last century originated, and such are those who are alone fit to enjoy and to possess it. If this should by chance meet the eye of the owner of the house to which I allude, I would wish him to know that half of the great pleasure which I took in visiting him was due to the sense that house and master were in perfect harmony, and I could say nothing more complimentary to either.

The reader will have thought the cupboard already too commodious of material, nevertheless I must note still a few more characteristics of it.

It has been the fashion, set by invaluable writers of the utmost eminence, to limit to the Gothic styles certain characteristics which are essential to all good architectural art; and it is necessary to insist sometimes on points which, but for the prejudices thus created, would be sufficiently obvious—points indeed better felt than explained. Elasticity, reticence, concentration, variety;—all these are primary conditions of a good style of architecture, and are all present in that which we are discussing. As we saw with regard to the mediæval styles, the essential spirit of the art is mainly apparent in the less monumental features. So to those whose ideas of eighteenth-century architecture are mainly deduced from the frequently severe exteriors—whence they derive an idea of monotony and of rigidity—features like the present should be specially instructive, since they point to a style thoughtful for and adaptable to the infinitesimal requirements of domestic life; a style

NEW ROMNEY.

which made use of such points of more elaborate design as gave a note of completeness and finish to what would otherwise be unattractive, however refined, but was content to employ them modestly and without ostentatious display; thus fulfilling the several conditions we noted above.

The bold, dignified tower of New Romney Church is, as we have seen, of Norman date. The remainder of the church is mainly of the fourteenth century, and somewhat monotonous and commonplace in character. The windows are nearly all of the type known as reticulated, which is perhaps the most common of all types in all parts of the country, and varies infinitely in merit according to the method of the treatment in detail. That in New Romney Church is of a very inferior type; nor

SEDILIA IN NEW-ROMNEY CHURCH.

is there much else to note in the church except the arrangement of the east end. The chancel, which has three aisles, had formerly three altars, of all of which the sedilia and piscinæ remain. In two, these are made in the solid stone screens which separate the central from the side chancel-

TOMB IN NEW ROMNEY CHURCH.

aisles, of one of which an illustration is given, and are in both cases precisely similar, each having a little piscina with a cusped ogee head, three stepped sedilia, and a hagioscope. A tomb of somewhat unusual character is also given.

Not much in Lydd is worthy of notice except the church, which, like that in Rye, is in an excellent state for the study of archæologists, containing as it does the distinct evidence of the treatment of various ages. The most remarkable features in it are of very late date, being the screens between the chancel aisles and the iron gateway to the priests' door, which are of uniform and very characteristic design. The screens are of oak; the skeleton door is partly of wrought, partly of cast iron, the construc-

IRON DOOR, LYDD.   WOOD WORK, LYDD.

tional *grille* being of the former, and the battlements and cusped arches filling the openings of the latter. Both are very good in effect.

The tower is of great height and very bold and effective in outline. The feature which is illustrated is of very fine design, and illustrates admirably a phase of Gothic architecture which should always be borne in mind in forming a comparative estimate of the Gothic styles. Whatever may be said in favour of the popular preference for the earlier periods of Gothic in respect of detail, it is certain that mediæval buildings show a constantly progressive grasp and power of producing continuity in design. In the present instance, the double doorway and four-light

WEST DOOR, LYDD.

window are admirably combined in one design, which is very definitely isolated by the depth of the jamb-mouldings. Those who are familiar with the best of the Warwickshire churches and with their paragon, St. Michael's, Coventry, will recall many an example of the same continuity of design, by which arcade and clerestory are united in one uninterrupted composition. The door to the belfry-staircase in the same tower has been added as a characteristic example of mediæval joinery.

BELFRY-DOOR, LYDD.

Ivychurch, of which the admirable early fifteenth-century stall-work is illustrated, is on the way homewards; but we may as well notice it out of its due turn, as no better place is to be found than the top of the tower of Lydd Church from which to take a farewell view of the Marsh. Besides the stall-work, its most noteworthy feature is an hexagonal beacon-tower, said to have been built as a landmark in the marshes, probably at a time when they were boggy and unsafe. The church inside is a very spacious one, far more so than the neighbourhood seems ever to have required. Indeed, one of its aisles is screened off as a school-room, and the greater part of its area is without seats. Not only here but throughout the Marsh, notwithstanding the ruin of very many churches, the accommodation appears to be greatly in excess of the worshippers, and this characteristic is common to lands recovered from the sea. Possibly for some such reason as this, which I suggest with all deference; that the land recovered from the sea became the property of the feudal lord of the adjoining territory, who made it over to those by whom it

STALLS AT IVYCHURCH.

had been redeemed or drained in consideration of certain fees, which he expended in the building of churches. Such foundations in the middle ages had probably more often a sacrificial than a practical origin.

Lydd spire was the most distant point discernible from Playden Hill from which we first viewed the Marsh. From it Playden Hill and Rye and Winchelsea and the Fairlight Hills are barely seen in the grey distance, just to be distinguished from the continuous low line of hills which form the limits of the original bay. Between us and them, lying somewhat off to the left, is much of the shore most lately recovered, in which the natural processes of transformation are still incomplete. On the other side is the constantly accumulating promontory of Dungeness, inhospitable both to men and ships. New Romney Church lies further inland, half hidden by a few trees; and beyond on all sides are little insular-looking clumps, containing a hamlet or village, and dotting the flat, unvaried extent of the marsh-land : thus vividly recalling at least the era of occasional floods, if not the archipelago stage of the Marsh's existence. Then on the other side is the sea, dotted not much more sparsely with ships in sail. The ships look so permanent and so much at home, and the hamlets so isolated, in such need to draw up and protect themselves by trees and stacks, that a touch of magic, so it seems, would set the hamlets sailing and fix the ships in permanence as islands, and the change would not be so very great after all. But the vision of the little group of graves at the foot of the tower, where lie the victims of the wreck of the *Northfleet*, dispels such dreams with a wholesome sense of preference for dry land, even the dry land of a marsh.

CONCLUSION.

TO carry something of the art of the past into the future is, perhaps, the best which we of this generation may hope to accomplish. The conditions under which we live are constantly teaching us this lesson, if we would learn it; and the self-confidence of the age is for ever crying out against such a limit to its ambition. For the first time, probably, in the world's history, we are left without any such central, continuous impulse and tendency as has hitherto carried forward the lamp of art through constant change, from generation to generation and from age to age. For the first time we stand aside and look upon all the phases of art-creation as things remote from ourselves, to be judged dispassionately and weighed one against another. We have no part in them, nor in any one of them, nor they in us. They are subjects for discussion, definition, analysis; things to be preferred or fancied, to be consciously and deliberately accepted or rejected. It is easier for a discursive age to criticise than to invent, to produce formulæ than design; and criticism is apt to flourish when artistic impulse languishes. For art lives in the absence of self-consciousness, and the best work has always been done without taking thought; moreover, the elements of which art mainly consists are delicate and minute, and are apt to evade the coarse machinery of words. Further, the influence of an analytic age upon art-production is injurious, in so far as it leads the artist to derive his impulse from current theories, thereby imparting to his work that *doctrinaire* character which is so commonly discernible in the works of many of the most able men of our day and generation; or, worse still, to adopt as his material ideas whose proper medium of expression is other than that of art. This, then, is the difficulty of the position: that in an age which is above all things critical, criticism in its more usual form is apt to have an injurious influence upon art.

By far the most important means of solving this problem of the time is to do good practical work, which may be the embodiment of ideas however subtle, however unconsciously held; and this, the sole and universal expression of the past, can hardly be over-valued in the present. But the age in which we live is above all things discursive, and will never be content with an exclusively practical exposition of its aims; and even though theory and analysis are repugnant to the artist, and possibly, for the time, injurious to his art, still it must be remembered that the theory of the present, if only it be founded upon real and genuine insight, may be translated into feeling in the future; and it is feeling alone which is the true material of art. Criticism, therefore, still has its own proper sphere, and may well be the handmaid of practical art, and assist it in bridging the void of the present and carrying the past into the future.

But to accomplish this purpose it must change its form, must surrender somewhat of its judicial and analytic character, and become passive and sympathetic. It must aim mainly at aiding the assimilation of those elements of character, poetry and sentiment of past times, which are to be the material of future success. And the method must vary with the conditions of the special branch of art. The study and criticism of architecture has its own proper and special conditions. A building can never be like a picture, complete within the limits of its frame and independent of influences beyond. It must be studied upon its own site, and under all the conditions of history, landscape, and neighbourhood.

The characteristic tendency towards centralisation and analysis leads us, for the most part, to arrange the vestiges of the past in museums, and to catalogue them in handbooks and '*Dictionnaires raisonnés.*' Such a treatment of them is economical of time and trouble both to the curiosity-hunter and to the theorist, but is apt to strip the objects so treated of the peculiar charm which lies in unbroken association and harmonious surroundings. Much light, too, is often thrown even upon the theoretic value of architectural works by a full appreciation of the relations between one work and another of the same neighbourhood; so that, whether it be theory that we seek, or the more fugitive charm of sentiment, it is best to take the wider view, and to open the mind to the full harmony of the combined influences of the locality.

Of the various phases of the architecture of the past it is as yet undecided which shall be ultimately established as the starting-point for the future. At the present moment there are almost as many rival factions as there are ancient styles, and the advantage seems to rest now with one, now with another. Meanwhile many of those who best appreciate the conditions of modern art are seen to use as precedents for their work examples the most diverse, and to found their practice upon the widest appreciation of the past. Future experience may draw closer the limits of their choice of precedents which they shall directly follow; but the essential elements of beauty, in virtue of which all the varied styles of former times have attained to success, must always be perceived by the artist who would enter into the full inheritance of the past: and for this reason also, his study must be wide and catholic.

Some such ideas as these have been the motive of the present essay, which is worth anything only so far as it succeeds in arresting something of the colour and sentiment of a time more favourable to art, now on all sides melting away, and so helps to carry something of the past into the art of the future.